2020 DIGITAL CHURCH STRATEGY

How Churches Can Use the
Internet to Expand Their Reach
& Glorify God

Alicia Wyman

TABLE OF CONTENTS

INTRODUCTION

Beloved Churches,

You should be using the internet to help you accomplish your mission.

Organizations have been putting their information online since 1990 and engaging with their online audiences since the mid-2000s. Although it can feel intimidating initially, having an online presence has been proven to be **more effective** and **less expensive** than traditional communication methods.

In this book, you will learn how to expand your church's reach online while still glorifying God. There is no reason to be afraid of platforms that were designed to help you become more efficient! There will **always** be a group of people who misuse the web (cyber-bullies, stalkers, etc.), but let's get caught using it to spread the Gospel and connect with His Body!

First, let's address the primary reasons why there is often a lack of people going to church:

- **Their Schedule or Lifestyle Makes It Difficult**
  - Missionaries, disabled-persons, night-shift workers, etc.
- **They Want To Learn Of Him Prior To Committing**

- "Come to our building" vs "We'll come to you"
- **They Want Engagement Outside of Sundays**
  - Ministry is 24/7, not 1 day a week
- **They Want Authentic Engagement**
  - -vs- 'Fake' Church or 'Cult' Experiences
- **They Feel They Can't Afford Church 'Quotas'**
  - -vs- The ability to cheerfully give
- **They Feel Judged & Pressured**
  - -vs- Loved & Allowed to genuinely grow
- **They Want The Message**
  - -vs- Lengthy services that often take a while to begin the sermon or 'meat' that they desperately came for
- **They Enjoy The Accessibility & Speed Of The Internet**
  - An uplifting word available at 2:00 AM when they're distraught

Of course we desire to meet prospective & current members of the Body in person. However, there is now a way to also meet with them digitally and still have (if not greater of) an impact.

And, it isn't antithetical to Christianity if some do not/cannot make it to your church's physical experience. **Adapt for them.**

God is, and always has been, challenging His church to operate more outside of their buildings, just as He sent His Son to demonstrate. Even if someone never visits your sanctuary, but gets saved because they received the Gospel online, Heaven rejoices!

Acts 1:21 reminds us that "...**Jesus went in and out among us**".
Our Lord repeatedly set the example of prioritizing meeting others where THEY are.
It's time to both implement & enjoy a healthy digital strategy for your church.

Let's glorify God with technology!

With love,

Alicia Wyman

STYLE GUIDE

Consistency is key with your branding so every church should have a style guide. A **style guide** is a set of standards for the formatting and design of your content.

You want to be both remembered & alluring with your marketing as opposed to having 50 different fonts & color schemes! Don't put more work on yourself every time you begin a new marketing project.

Your style guide's elements will ultimately echo that of your church's current branding (your logo & so on). However, without fully rebranding, you should craft a style guide for your marketing designs that will **evoke certain emotions**.

Colors

You'll want to choose one color to be your **primary**, one your **secondary**, and no more than three as **accents**.

- Red
  - **Positive** - energy, excitement, passion, love, wealth, good luck, power, security
  - **Negative** - violence, anger
- Yellow
  - **Positive** - optimism, light, warmth, motivation, creativity, confidence
  - **Negative** - immaturity, distracting
- Blue

- ○ **Positive** - trust, partnership, all-inclusive
- ○ **Negative** - freezing, cold-heartedness, common
- Orange
  - ○ **Positive** - bold, activity, productivity, vitality, fun, playfulness
  - ○ **Negative** - glaring/gaudy
- Green
  - ○ **Positive** - nature, easy to look at, wealth, health, prestige, serenity, refreshing, outdoors, safety
  - ○ **Negative** - illness, envious, greedy
- Purple
  - ○ **Positive** - sophistication, royalty, positivity, trust, value, bravery, secure
  - ○ **Negative** - conceit/pompousness
- Pink
  - ○ **Positive** - feminine, romantic
  - ○ **Negative** - fragility, overly-cautious
- Brown
  - ○ **Positive** - earthlike, natural, simplistic, durable
  - ○ **Negative** - dirty, primitive, cheap
- Black
  - ○ **Positive** - prestige, value, timelessness, sophistication
  - ○ **Negative** - death, grief, rebellion
- White
  - ○ **Positive** - purity, soft, clean, nobility, birth
  - ○ **Negative** - plain, unoriginal, sterility, distance

You'll want to save your color selections as hex code colors.

Hex code colors are universal colors used in displaying web pages on the internet and are expressed in six-digit combinations of numbers and letters defined by their mix of red, green, and blue (RGB). Each hex code stands for a specific shade and begins with a # symbol.

For example:

- #000000 = **Black**
- #FA1782 = Deep Pink
- #0857C3 = Royal Blue

Try using **Color Space** to easily generate beautiful color palettes that come with hex codes!

Shapes

Choose up to three shapes that best illustrate the mission of your church.

- **Circles** - community, friendship, love, complete, perfection
- **Ovals** - sturdiness, endurance, stability
- **Squares & Rectangles** - power, strength, professionalism, efficiency, stability
- **Vertical Lines** - strength, masculinity, energy
- **Horizontal Lines** - calmness, tranquility, balance, protection, settled
- **Angled Lines** - movement, energy, speed
- **Curved Lines** - feminine, happiness, generosity, rhythm

Fonts

Select fonts for your **title, headers, subheaders,** and **normal text**. Try using <u>**Google Fonts**</u> and sorting each of the **Categories** by **Most Popular**.

- **Serif**
    - **Feels**: traditional, authoritative, formal, respected, reliable
    - **Examples**: Merriweather, Roboto Slab, Playfair Display, Lora
- **Sans Serif**
    - **Feels**: trustworthy, straight-forward, sophisticated, modern, clean, universal, humanist
    - **Examples**: Montesserat, Lato, Oswald, Raleway
- **Handwriting**
    - **Feels**: elegant, creative, personal, whimsical, stylish
    - **Examples**: Dancing Script, Caveat, Permanent Marker, Satisfy
- **Display**
    - **Feels**: prominent, amusing, expressive, friendly, embellished
    - **Examples**: Lobster, Abril Fatface, Righteous, Monoton
- **Monospace**
    - **Feels**: legible, code-based, techy
    - **Examples**: Inconsolata, Nanum Gothic Coding, VT323, Nova Mono

EXERCISE #1

Craft an emotion-evoking style guide for your church.

COLOR SCHEME		
Primary Color		
Secondary Color		
Accent Color 1		
Accent Color 2		
Accent Color 3		
SHAPE PSYCHOLOGY		
Shape 1		
Shape 2		
Shape 3		
FONT STYLES		
Title	Size: 21+ pt	
Headers	Size: 18-20 pt	
Subheaders	Size: 13-17 pt	
Normal Text	Size: 10-12 pt	

SEO & KEYWORD RESEARCH

The next most important task of a digital church strategy is keyword research which is used to enhance your Search Engine Optimization.

A **search engine,** like Google or YouTube, is an online database software that indexes sites based on **keywords** or **keyphrases** (informative words used to indicate what content is on a site). **Search Engine Optimization (SEO)** is the process of improving the quality and quantity of your website's traffic by increasing its visibility to users of an online search engine. **Keyword Research** is identifying possible search terms that people enter into search engines while looking for specific content.

For instance, if I go to a **search engine** online like Google and type in the **keyword** 'seo' or the **keyphrase** 'what is seo', the search engine will then display a handful of sites, videos, etc. that pertain to what I searched for. Sites that contain content that exactly match what I searched for are said to be **search engine optimized**. You can find out which words people are using the most by doing **keyword research** and using those **keywords** on your websites, social media platforms, etc.

So, if your research reveals that more people are searching for the keyword 'seo' over 'search engine optimization' or 'how to seo', then you would include 'seo' on your sites to ensure that they pop up at the top of the search engine's results.

Give the people what they want.

You can perform keyword research via two methods: **search engine suggestions** or **keyword research software**. You can also find tools in the **RESOURCES** section of this book.

Search Engine Suggestions

Head to a search engine (Google or YouTube) and type in **the keyword or keyphrase that primarily represents your content.**

For example, if you're posting your sermon about 'depression' online, then type in the word 'depression'. The search engine will then scan its database for content containing that keyword, and begin to offer you its most popular suggestions. You can then use some of these keyphrases in your content.

Keyword Research Software

Perform **more advanced research** by using a software designed to deep dive into keyword usage statistics.

You can use a free software like **Keywordtool.io** to accomplish this.

EXERCISE #2

Plan your keyword research strategy below.

What word best identifies your content?	
RESEARCH METHOD	
Search Engine Suggestions	☐
-or-	
Keyword Research Software	☐
RESEARCH	
Keywords	
Keyphrases	

WEBSITES

Ah, the website. Your digital church 'building'.

Many churches make the unfortunate mistake of using their websites as a **résumé** (all about their church) as opposed to a **resource** (what their church can do for others).

Your website should primarily serve new eyes & potential members. Your internal congregation can benefit from some of the information, but it's more so a center for general information, FAQs, & the message of the Gospel.

Let's get started.

Creation

You can easily build & maintain a website on your own nowadays! However, hiring someone else to do so for you is still a viable option. Just be sure to tell them that you want it to reflect the structure that you're about to learn of.

The best website builder of 2020 is **Wix**.

You can build a website on its platform for free, however, I suggest upgrading to the **Pro** version which is currently $22 per month. This will give you extra storage, an events calendar, & so much more.

Main Menu & Pages

Remember, your website should **serve your viewers & visitors**.

It's easy to try and make everything a priority for your website, but, let's keep the amount of main pages in your navigation menu at 7 or less. Any additionally necessary pages can go under-the-wing of a main page as a subpage.

In order, the only main pages you'll need are:

1. **Home**
2. **Plan A Visit** or **I'm New Here**
3. **About**
4. **Sermons**
5. **Youth**
6. **Get Involved**
7. **Give**

NOTE: You wouldn't utilize a Sermons page if you aren't yet video or audio recording your sermons.

NOTE: NOWHERE on your website should you include a slider or 'image carousel'. Users ignore them and they slow your page. Choose 1 image to be the focal point whenever you're adding images.

Home

Above-the-fold on your website's homepage (before a viewer would need to start scrolling), you'll need to include the following information:

- **Logo & Church Name**
- **Main Menu**
- **Headline**
  - A phrase that tells them 'what's in it for them' if they choose to be a part of your church
- **Plan A Visit or I'm New Here Button**
  - Linked to your Plan A Visit or I'm New Here page
- **Church Service Times**
- **Church Address**
- **Inspirational Image**
  - One that evokes the emotion you would want them to feel if they visited
  - Covers the majority of the screen

Here are a couple of examples:

After-the-fold, your homepage should include your:

- **Vision Statement**
- **Mission Statement**
- **A Summary of the Gospel**
- **Phone Number**
- **Fax Number** (optional)
- **Email Address**
- **Church Address**
- **Google Map**
  - With your church address pinned
- **Question Form** (optional)
  - Linked to an appropriate email address

Plan A Visit or I'm New Here

This is the page where potential members can get **an overview of what it's like to attend one of your services**. This page must include:

- **A Response to Possible Objections**
    - A few sentences acknowledging new visitor fears and that you empathize with their feelings
    - For example: *"We know that visiting a new church can be nerve-wrecking, confusing, or maybe even terrifying. We want to make sure your experience with us is as inviting as possible."*
- **Service Times**
- **Church Address**
- **Google Map**
    - With your church address pinned
- **What Can I Expect?**
    - A short paragraph explaining the typical agenda & service length as not everyone knows what it's like to attend church
    - Did I mention the service length? Don't skip that. They want to know.
- **What About My Kids?**
    - People are protective of their children so include a summary of your different youth departments, how youth are split up, safety, what they'll be learning, the check-in experience, when & where parents should take them or if they'll get dismissed instead, etc.

- **Testimonials**
  - Include at least 3 testimonials from real, diverse people from your church along with their photos

About

On this page you'll want to include your church's:

- **Vision Statement**
- **Mission Statement**
- **History**
- **Staff Information**
  - Names
  - Contact Information
  - Bios (optional)

Youth

Your Youth page must feature:

- **An Introduction**
  - A few sentences about the ages &/or grades levels you serve, the divisions they are in, & the experience they will have
  - For example: *"At Faith Church, youth ages 0-17 years will experience a safe, age appropriate environment where they will learn about Jesus in a creative and relevant way. Youth either go to the Nursery, Elementary, or Teen groups."*
- **Your First Visit**
  - Cover what to expect during check-in, where it is, & how it works

- **Meet Our Youth Director(s)**
    - Include a photo, contact information, & a short quote from them about their excitement to meet the youth
- **Our [Nursery]**
    - Cover where infants would go
- **Our [Elementary Area]**
    - Cover where kids would go
- **Our [Teen Area]**
    - Cover where older youth would go
- **Parent's Viewing Room/Baby Lounge**
    - If your church has a quiet room for parents who are nursing or don't want to take their child to the youth groups, then mention that too and where it's located
- **Pre-Registration Form**
    - If you're able to sync up an online form with your current check-in system, then allow parents to pre-register their kids to save them time
    - Be sure that it immediately sends them a 'Form Completion' email of some kind

Sermons

Prospective visitors want to know what you are preaching and what your messages are like! If you were a business, your sermon would be the 'product' you were selling. **They want to know everything about it before they buy**.

Even if your website isn't able to hold all of your video/audio files (most cannot), then still use a Sermons page to list their titles in descending order with links to where each one is stored (on YouTube, Vimeo, etc.)

You'll also want to **create a naming system for your titles** for easier locating.

Here's an example:

Sermon Name | Series Name | Speaker Name
MONTH DD, YYYY
Watch/Listen Now: [video link]

Seasons of Depression | Mental Health & God | Pastor John Doe
January 1, 2020
Watch/Listen Now: randomvideolink.com

Get Involved

Finally, the page where all of your **events & internal information** goes!

On this page you will include a calendar or list of:

- **Your Services**
- **Your Bible Studies**
- **Your Small Groups**
- **Your Church Events**

If you're using a list, put your repetitive events (service times, Bible studies, & small groups) at the top of the page, then list your remaining events afterwards. This way, you won't need to repeat them and they will always rest up top leaving the rest of your page for the come-and-go events.

For example:

- **Service Times** - Sundays 10:00 AM & 12:00 PM
- **Bible Study** - Tuesdays 5:30 PM-7:00 PM
- **Men's Group** - Saturdays 1:00 PM-3:00 PM
- **Women's Group** - Saturdays 1:00 PM-3:00 PM
- **Youth Group** - Saturdays 3:30 PM-5:00 PM
- *[Remainder of page used for non-recurring events such as revivals, picnics, ceremonies, holiday services, etc.]*

Give

Many churches overload their visitors & members with far too many 'cool' giving options.

Studies continue to show that church-goers prefer to use:

- **In-Person Baskets**
  - For cash & checks
- **Your Website's Giving Page**
  - EASILY accessible by anyone with a smartphone
  - No app download or text opt-in required
- **Your Lobby Kiosk** (optional)
  - For those with a credit card, but no smartphone

Your Give page should feature a **Multi-Step form**.

Humans are easily overwhelmed by long forms in general. Think about paper tax forms!

So instead of one long page, put everything into separate sections so that they can only see that section before moving on to the next. Be sure to ask for the less-sensitive information first (*"How much do you want to give?"*) and save their card information for last.

If your existing church management software doesn't feature a payment processor, try using a software like **Typeform,** which uses a payment processor called **Stripe** to help you securely accept payments. Create a form and feature it on your Give page.

Footer

Last, although certainly not least, your website's footer. This is **the real estate at the bottom of your site that is visible on every page**, just like your main menu up top.

The footer is where you can literally add whatever your heart desires, but people often neglect it! You'll usually only see their copyright information there...

Here are some things that you can feature in your website footer. I suggest using all of them if you can.

- **Search Bar**
  - Not everyone knows your site back-and-forth like you do
- **Mission Statement**
- **Social Media Links**
- **Service Times**

- The more you repeat it, the better
- **Church Address**
- **Phone Number**
- **Email Address**

Site Performance

Lastly, **ensure that your website is optimized,** loading fast, and up-to-par with search engine preferences. Use some of the website performance tools from the **RESOURCES** section to run a few tests.

EXERCISE #3

Plan out your website strategy below. Give this to your web designer if you're hiring one.

CREATION				
Wix	☐	-or-	Hire Someone	☐

HOME PAGE (above-the-fold)				
Logo & Church Name	☐			
Headline/Vision Statement				
Plan A Visit Button	☐	-or-	I'm New Here Button	☐
Church Service Times				
Church Address				
Inspirational Image	☐			

HOME PAGE (after-the-fold)	
Vision Statement	
Mission Statement	
A Summary of the Gospel	
Phone Number	
Fax Number	
Email Address	
Church Address	
Google Map Address Link	
Question Form	☐

PLAN A VISIT -or- I'M NEW HERE PAGE	
Response to Possible Objections	
Service Times	
Church Address	
Google Map Address Link	
What Can I Expect?	
What About My Kids?	
Testimonial Person 1	
Testimony 1	
Testimonial Person 2	

Testimony 2	
Testimonial Person 3	
Testimony 3	

ABOUT PAGE	
Vision Statement	
Mission Statement	
Church History	
Lead Pastor Info	

Pastor's Assistant Info	
Associate Pastor Info	
Administrative Assistant Info	
Worship Leader Info	
Youth Director Info	
Staff Member Info	
Staff Member Info	
Staff Member Info	

Staff Member Info	
Staff Member Info	
Staff Member Info	

YOUTH PAGE	
Introduction	
Your First Visit	
Meet Our Youth Director(s)	

Our [Nursery]	
Our [Elementary Area]	
Our [Teen Area]	
Parent's Viewing Room/Baby Lounge	
Pre-Registration Form	

SERMONS PAGE	
Can you include this page at this time?	☐
Sermon Name | Series Name | Speaker Name | Date	☐
-or-	
Sermon Name - Series Name - Speaker Name - Date	☐

GET INVOLVED PAGE	
Service Times	
Bible Study Info	
Groups Info	

Other Events	

GIVE PAGE

This page is pretty self-explanatory.

*Just make sure that your designer knows that you want **a multi-step form that safely accepts payments.***

FACEBOOK

Facebook is the #1 **social networking site and makes it easy for you to connect and share with others online.** Currently, Facebook has nearly 2.5 billion active users and is a great platform to promote your organization & connect with your members.

Most organizations get Facebook all wrong. Similar to their websites, they use their Facebook page as a **résumé** rather than a **resource**. **Marketing isn't about you**. It's about your potential member, how they feel, what they're looking for, and what you & God can offer them.

You'll want to take advantage of most of the different options available to you on Facebook. Let's dissect the critical ones:

- **Pages**
  - Serve your prospective audience by providing general information for them to learn about your organization
- **Groups**
  - Serve your internal audience through conversations & internal announcements
- **Events**
  - Market them to both your prospective & internal audiences
- **Ads**
  - Advertise desired events and employment/volunteer opportunities

Pages

Creation

In order to create a Facebook page for your organization, you'll first need a personal Facebook profile. To create one, go to **Facebook** and follow the instructions.

Then, to create a business page, (on a desktop) go to the top header menu and click **Create**, then **Page** from it's dropdown options. On the new screen, choose **Business or Brand**. Enter your **Page Name** (your church name) and a **Category** (**church** or **religious organization**). Skip the profile and cover photos for now.

Next, go up top and open the page **Settings**.

Tabs

In your Settings, change your page from Standard to Business by going to **Templates & Tabs > Edit Current Template > Business > Apply Template**.

Then change:

- **Use Default Tabs > OFF**
- **Reorder Tabs**
  - Home
  - About
  - Reviews
  - Events
  - Groups

- Posts
- Videos
- Photos
- Community
- **Turn Off Offers Tab**

Settings

The other settings you'll want to make are:

- **General**
  - Visitor Posts = Disable
  - Page Updates = Disable
- **Page Info**
- **Messaging**
  - Starting a Messenger Conversation = ON
    - Use the **Add Personalization** feature to include their information
    - Message Idea:

> Hi, [**First Name of Recipient**].
>
> Thanks for contacting us and please send us any questions you may have!
>
> Church Name
> Website
> Phone Number
> Email Address
> Church Address

- o Add Messenger to your website
  - ▪ Although you can do this at any time. You'll want to embed into your site's HTML, so have someone who knows about coding/web development assist you.
  - o Set up automated responses
- **Page Roles** (for teams)
  - o Admin   (Page owners including you)
  - o Editor   (Similar to Admin but cannot change Page settings or manage roles)
  - o Moderator (can manage your posts, messages, & ads)
  - o Advertiser (can manage ads)
  - o Analyst (View insights, view Page quality tab, & see who published as the Page)
  - o Jobs Manager (can create and manage jobs & ads)

About Tab & Story Section

Back on your Facebook **page**, click on the **About** tab and fill in your organization's information.

Afterwards, use **Our Story** section to the right of the screen to give a longer overview of your organization's information. This could literally contain the exact information from your About page of your website. This section could also be used as a press release so be sure to include some photos & contact information!

Profile Photo

Now for the fun stuff. Your graphic elements.

*NOTE: Be sure to check out the **RESOURCES** section in this book for perfectly sized templates for all graphic elements!*

Your Facebook **profile photo** should be of your church's logo and be 170 x 170 pixels in size.

Cover Photo

Your **cover photo** should be similar (or even identical) to the above-the-fold image on your website and be 820 x 360 pixels in size.

In the visible area (640 x 312 px) of your cover photo, make sure that you include your logo and headline.

The photo also needs to **show human faces** (preferably of real members/staff) and evoke a positive emotion. This way, visitors will immediately see how visiting your church will make them feel before scrolling down the rest of your profile. **Set the tone**.

Button

Your page's **call-to-action button** will tell your visitors what you would like them to do. The two best call-to-action options for churches are:

- **Learn More** - sends them to your website
- **Visit Group** - sends them to your congregation's Facebook Group

To edit your this button:

- Hover over the call-to-action button below your page's cover photo and select **Edit Button**
- Change to **Learn More** or **Visit Group**
- Click **Finish**

Posts

Posts to your Facebook page ought to be **essential & minimal**.

Remember, **your page & website mimic the first time experience of a physical visit**, so don't overwhelm your digital visitors with internal or unnecessary information when they haven't gotten to know you yet.

For example, when visitors walk into your physical church, do you shake their hand and say, "Join us for our potluck tonight at 3:00 PM!", then walk away?...

Or do you introduce yourself, welcome them, and ask if they need any help?

One way makes it about you, and the other way makes it about them.

So, keep your posts limited to **general information** like service time changes, staff changes, your latest sermon links, or your latest sermon series. And, **your sermon series post should ALWAYS be pinned to the top of your page** so viewers can immediately see what your church is currently teaching. However, if there is another urgent general announcement (like service time changes, [COVID-19] information, or an available job), then post that to the top instead for a while.

The captions on your sermon & sermon series posts should have an alluring effect. If you were selling a product, you would draw in a customer by addressing:

- **A Pain Point**
    - What problem do they have? What answer are they looking for? Why should they pay attention to you instead of other advertisers?
    - Ex: *"Have you been feeling depressed lately?", "Are you looking for a local volunteer opportunity?"*
    - A bit of keyword research could help you with this
- **Your Solution/Product**
    - Ex: *"Watch Pastor John's latest sermon 'Joy in the Morning' and learn how to overcome it today."*
- **How They Can (Easily) Obtain It From You**
    - Ex: *"Click here to watch it now: www.randomvideolink.com"*

Lastly, **you can schedule posts** to be released at a later time. I use this feature to batch schedule posts to release for the remainder of the year! This saves me so much time as opposed to trying to post everyday.

To do this, select **Schedule** (or the clock icon) instead of **Post** once you've created a post. You can also do this in your **Publishing Tools** which is located in the horizontal menu at the top of your page.

Stories

Stories are temporary (usually 24 hour) photo and video posts designed to share your experiences. But, since it is designed to engage viewers in a personal as opposed to general way, we won't be using stories on our church Facebook pages.

However, feel free to use them in your Facebook Groups and on Instagram where you have the freedom to be more specific and engaging.

Jobs

Job posts on your Facebook **page** should follow a beautiful structure so that potential candidates get the most out of it. Skip ahead to the **INDEED** section to learn how to craft one.

To post a **Job** to Facebook:

1. Above **Write a post...** at the top of your Page's timeline, click **Job**
2. Add details to your post
3. You can also add **Additional Questions** if you want to ask applicants more questions
4. If you'd like to receive job applications by email instead of your **page** messages inbox, scroll

down to the bottom and enter your email
address under **Receive Applications By Email**
5. On the right, click **Desktop News Feed** or
   Mobile News Feed to see what your job post
   looks like on different devices
6. Click **Publish Job Post**

Alternatively, you can post jobs in a normal page post with a detailed caption and a post-sized image.

For example:

- **Caption**
  - Job Title | Salary | Organization Name
  - A url link to the job on Indeed.com
- **Image**
  - 1080 x 1080 pixels
  - Showing one of the job's responsibilities

Groups

Groups are a place to directly engage with your congregation. This is the opposite of your Facebook Page, as it allows you to be more open and even fun!

You really only need one Facebook group for your congregation members.

However, if your church has multiple locations, then you'll want one for each. If you absolutely must create another group for a smaller sect of members (Women's Group, Men's Group, etc.), then at least limit the amount of excess **groups** to 3.

Creation

To create a group:

- Click **Create** in the top right of Facebook then select **Group**
- **Name Your Group**
  - Similar to page name
  - Ex: *Faith Church Members or Members of Faith Church*
- **Add Some People**
  - Skip this for now
- **Select Privacy**
  - Private
- **Hide Group**
  - Visible
- Click **Create**

Settings

Open your group **Settings** by hovering over the **More** icon just under the group cover photo. Then, select **Edit Group Settings**.

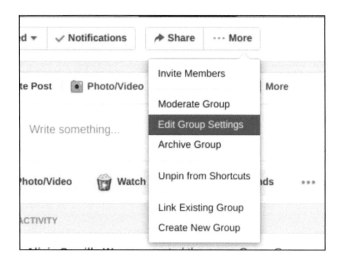

You'll then want to edit:

- **Description**
  - A good one is *"Use this group to engage with us beyond Sundays!"*
- **Location**
- **Tags**
  - For now, just use your City, State
- **Color**
- **Web Address**
- **Membership Approval**
  - Only admins and moderators
- **Membership Requests from Pages**
  - Don't Allow
- **Posting Permissions**
  - Only Admins
- **Post Approval**
  - Enabled

Then click **Save**.

Moderate Group

In the tabbed menu to the left of the page, click on **Moderate Group**.

Then Edit:

- **Topics For Posts**
    - This allows group members find the information they're interested in and you should use them to categorize every post you create as well
    - A few starter topics you can use are *Announcements, Prayer Requests, Praise Reports, & Engage With Us*
- **Create Rules**
    - Use the sample rules and/or your own
- **Automatic Member Approvals**
    - You can edit this later, but it helps if you don't have the time to manually approve new members each day
    - A good question would be, *"Are you a member of [Solid Rock] Church?"*

Cover Photo

Your **group cover photo** should include your church's logo, the group's name, and be 1640 x 856 pixels in size.

NOTE: Only about 1640 x 664 pixels of the cover photo will show so keep everything within this parameter

Link to Your Facebook Page

In order to link your **group** to your organization's Facebook **page**, return to your Facebook **page** and on the left side menu, select **Groups**. Then select **Link Your Group**.

Posts

Although there are plenty of options to choose from, we'll focus on how to create a standard, engaging **post** for your group members.

Below are the components of an excellent post:

- **Caption**
    - For **alluring** posts, use the same strategy that you learn for your Facebook Page posts (*a pain point, your solution, how they can easily obtain it*)
    - For **engaging** posts, stay light-hearted and get to know your members by sparking interesting conversation (*Other than Jesus, who in the Bible would you love to have a conversation with? What was your favorite video game growing up?*)
- **Graphic**
    - Every post should have a **colored, scroll-stopping** aspect that obeys the **style guide** you chose in EXERCISE #1 (*at least the fonts & shapes as colors may need to change in a certain situation*)

- Background - displayed in colored or patterned squares below when you create a post; select one that enhances your caption
- Photo - add 1080 x 1080 pixel photo (*with or without words*) that supports your caption
- Gif or Video - add a short & sweet one that supports your caption
- **URL Link (optional)**
  - If you need to send them to another site/page
- **Topic**
  - Any of the **Post Topics** that you created earlier

You should be posting something **DAILY** and typically in the **afternoon or evening** (between 1:00 PM-6:00 PM) unless the adverse is necessary. I told you the Schedule Post feature would come in handy...

The types of posts you should be creating could follow this schedule:

*NOTE: Remember, marketing isn't about you. **Only 1 post per week should promote your Sunday service.** Use the other days to genuinely engage.*

- Monday - **Trigger Spiritual Practice**
  - *"Take 30 seconds to pray for [someone/something] today."*
  - *"What's something you're grateful for today?"*

- Tuesday - **Reading & Learning Scripture Together**
    - A 'mini-sermon' (3 quick points or less)
    - People wish they read the Bible more so use this time to help them learn and dissect
    - *"[Scripture Reference] says that [Scripture Verse] which means [Point 1] [Point 2] [Point 3]"*
- Wednesday - **Spiritual Question**
    - Allow your members to open up in a safe place
    - *"When did you first realize you wanted to follow Jesus?"*
    - *"What scripture do you turn to when you're feeling lost?"*
- Thursday - **Bible Facts**
    - *"Did you know that King David also…"*
    - *"Did you know that when Jesus returns…"*
    - *"Fun Fact: Heaven and Hell are…"*
- Friday - **Funday**
    - Keep it simple, fun, & slightly debatable!
    - *"Would you rather see one of Jesus' sermons or one of His miracles?"*
    - *"What topping does NOT belong on a pizza?"*
- Saturday - **Invitation**
    - Finally, invite everyone to tomorrow's church service and explain what will be taught
    - *"Tomorrow, you'll learn how to love difficult people. Feel free to invite a friend. We'll see you there!"*

- Sunday - **Service Experience**
  - Tell the story of what happened in service today
  - Try using: a quote from the speaker's sermon, a photo of a baptism, the look on a worshipper's tearful face, etc.

Events

Events let you create, organize, and respond to gatherings with people on Facebook.

Which To Create

Be sure to create [single or recurring] events for any gathering that your members should know about.

For example:

- **Church Service**
- **Bible Studies**
- **Large Events**
- **Small Group Classes/Gatherings**
- **Ministries to Serve In**

Creation

You can create an event by going to your Facebook page or group and:

- Clicking **Events** in the left menu
- Select **Create Event** on the left side
- Click **Create Public Event**
- Add a **cover photo or video**
  - Photo - 1200x628 pixels

- Video - between 30 seconds and 5
      minutes
- **Fill in** the information fields
- **Invite** guests

Ads

Boost Your Post

You can advertise your **events** with Facebook's easy to use **Boost Your Post** feature that's available for most posts.

On your Facebook page:

- Find the **post** or **event** you want to boost
- Select **Boost Post**
- **Fill in the details** for your ad
    - **Image & Text** - Facebook will automatically use the content from your post but ensure that the text-to-image ratio isn't too high & that your ad will runs smoothly with **Facebook's Text Overlay Tool**
    - **Audience** - Choose one of their recommended audiences or create a new audience based on specific traits
    - **Total Budget** - Select their recommended budget or create a custom budget
    - **Duration** - Select one of their suggested time frames or your own specific time frame
    - **Payment Method**

- When you're done, select **Boost**

Business Manager

When you're ready to use Facebook's in depth advertising tool, Facebook **Business Manager**, it will allow you to integrate your Facebook marketing endeavors across your business and with external partners.

You'll be able to:

- **Run and analyze your ads**
- **Manage assets like your Page and ad account**
- **Add an agency or marketing partner to help you manage it all**

Here's how to set it up:

- Go to **business.facebook.com/overview**
- Click **Create Account**
- Enter a name for your business, your name and work email address and click **Next**
- Enter your business details and click **Submit**

Learn how to maximize your use of this tool by visiting the **Facebook for Business Help Center**.

EXERCISE #4

Plan your Facebook marketing approach below.

PAGE	
Tab Reorder	☐
Settings	☐
About Tab Information	☐
Our Story Section	☐
Profile Photo	☐
Cover Photo	☐
Button	☐
Create Your First Page Post	☐
GROUP	
Settings	☐
Topics for Posts	☐
Create Group Rules	☐
Cover Photo	☐
Link to Facebook Page	☐
Create Your First Group	☐

Post	
EVENTS	
Service Times	☐
Bible Studies	☐
Small Groups	☐
Church Events	☐

INDEED

I won't need to go into too much detail here, but **Indeed** is the world's largest job posting website and offers great benefits for businesses of all sizes:

- Indeed **fills nearly twice as many job listings** than any other job posting website
- It has **more than 250 million visitor**s on their site each month so your job posts are likely to be viewed by qualified candidates
- It's **a place to elevate your organization & brand** so candidates can see if your organization is a good fit for them
- You can **run paid ads** (called Sponsored Posts) on the site for relevant & qualified candidates to see your job post up top no matter what they're searching for

Do some initial **keyword research** on the job/volunteer role you're posting and get a list of words ready to plug into your job/volunteer summary.

To create an Indeed account, go to **Indeed for Employers**. Then, edit your account **settings** and company **brand page** using detailed information and high-quality, emotion-evoking photos if possible.

When you're ready to post a job, be sure that it follows a beautiful structure that uses the **keywords** from your research.

Exercise #5 will help you form an excellent job post.

EXERCISE #5

INDEED JOB POST	
Job Title	
Brief Position Summary	
Organization Overview	
Job Responsibilities *Listed from most important to least important*	
Job requirements *Listed from most important to least important & if each is required or preferred*	

Shift & Hours *Mention any occasional hours*	
Salary/Range *Yes, they want to know this!*	

YOUTUBE

YouTube is second only to Google as the largest search engine in the world. People everywhere are looking for answers, education, & entertainment and they want it in the form of an easily digestible video.

It is INCREDIBLY easy to create and maintain a YouTube channel. **Be sure that video or at least audio or your messages are on this platform**. This way, the message of Jesus will be easily accessible which could save someone from anywhere in the world!

Create a Google Account

If you don't already have one for your organization, you'll need to create a **Google account** or a **Gmail** email in order to use YouTube.

Create one by going to **support.google.com/accounts**.

Be sure to add a 170 x 170 pixels account profile photo of your organization's logo.

Channel Setup

Setting up your **YouTube channel** is simple.

Check out the **YouTube Creator Academy's Quick Start Guide**.

Be sure to add a 2560 x 1440 pixels **channel banner cover photo**.

Filming

If you have an existing film setup for your church, then use that. And remember to **always use good lighting** and **an appropriate environment/background**.

If you're in need of a setup, here are a few different options:

- **Free**
  - ○ A smartphone or webcam that can film in 1080p resolution
- **Affordable**
  - ○ Canon EOS M50 Mirrorless Video Camera
    - ■ Currently $599 on Amazon
  - ○ BOYA BY-M1000 Condenser Microphone
    - ■ Currently $125 on Amazon
  - ○ BOYA BY-M1000 3.5mm Electret Condenser Microphone with 1/4" Adapter for Smartphones/iPhone/DSLR/Cameras
    - ■ Currently $19.88 on Amazon

Video Editing

- **Free**
  - ○ You can film straight through with **YouTube Live** if you'd like

- - **Blender** - available on Windows, Mac, and Linux
  - **Affordable**
    - **WeVideo** Unlimited Plan - $15.99/month and is also great for Chromebooks
  - **High-Quality**
    - **Adobe Premiere Pro** - $19.99/month with a 7-day free trial
    - Apple's **Final Cut Pro X** - $299.99 total with a 30-day free trial

Title

A good title is usually keyword-friendly and orderly, which will make them easier to find. Create a naming system for your video titles just like the way you learned how to do for the Sermon page of your website. However, you won't need to include the date or link, as YouTube will take care of it.

Try using one of these formats:

- **Sermon Name | Series Name | Speaker Name**
- **Sermon Name - Series Name - Speaker Name**

Thumbnail

A **YouTube video thumbnail** is the first thing viewers will see when they are browsing and trying to decide which video will give them the best answer to whatever it is they're looking for.

Your thumbnail should:

- **Be 1280 x 720 pixels in size**
- **Follow your style guide**
- **Include your logo**
- **Include the title or an alluring headline**
- **Include a background photo that shows**
  - The face of the speaker (preferably)
  - or something relative to the video content

There are resources for photo editing and royalty-free images in the **RESOURCES** section of this book.

Description

Your video's description should display good marketing by being **clear, organized, and attractive**.

A quality description will include:

- **Headline**
  - What pain point does your video aid?
- **Benefit**
  - How will your video help them?
- **Speaker Name & Title**
- **Main Scripture Reference**
- **Your Website Link**
  - Start with an http or https protocol
- **Your YouTube Channel Link**
  - Start with an http or https protocol
- **Your Social Media Links**
  - Start with an http or https protocol
- **About Information**

-      ○   1-2 sentences about your church or just use your mission & vision statements
- **Call-to-Action**
  - Ask viewers to like your video, subscribe to your channel, &/or stay tuned for future video releases.
- **Contact Information**
  - Church Address
  - Phone Number
  - Email Address
- **Relevant Hashtags**
  - Hashtags are used online to identify content on a specific topic
  - Always use hashtags for your church's name, speaker's name, and a keyword describing your video's topic

Here's an example:

> *Are you experiencing what feels like a hopeless struggle?*
> *In this video, you'll learn how to find hope and overcome any obstacle!*
>
> *SPEAKER: Pastor John Doe*
> *SCRIPTURE: Job 42:1-17*
>
> *WEBSITE: https://www.google.com*
> *YOUTUBE: https://www.youtube.com*
> *FACEBOOK: https://www.facebook.com*
> *INSTAGRAM: https://www.instagram.com*
>
>
> *----------------*
> *At Faith Church, we aim to help people discover their purpose.*
> *Subscribe to our channel and learn a new lesson every Sunday!*
>
> *1234 5th Avenue*
> *City, State Zip*
> *(888) 555-0101*
> *info@faithchurch.org*
>
> *#depression #faithchurch #pastorjohndoe*

Tags

Do some keyword research on what people who would want to watch your video are actively searching for so that you can add tags to your video. **Tags** are keywords you can add to your video on the backend that will help viewers find your content. You can also include your church name & speaker name.

While you're uploading a video, you'll see a **Tags** section where you can add them.

Uploading

You can now post your video or even schedule it to premiere at a later date. **Premieres** build anticipation around your video.

Also, when uploading your video, know that sometimes it could take a little while.

According to **YouTube's Help Center**, your video may upload slower due to:

- **File Type & Size**
  - Your video's file type and video format determine its size. To make your uploads faster, encode your videos in one of our recommended formats.
- **Slow Internet Connection**
  - Search "internet speed test" on **google.com** to check your internet connection. Slow or unstable internet connection is one of the main causes of slow uploads.
- **Heavy Uploads Traffic**
  - You might be uploading during a busy time. At some peak hours, your Internet

Service Provider registers spikes of upload traffic and might take longer to upload your video to YouTube. Find out more about video performance on YouTube.

- **Resolution**
    - ○ Higher resolution videos take longer to upload. For instance, a 4K video will take longer to upload than a 1080p video

EXERCISE #6

Ensure that your channel & videos are ready for YouTube!

Google Account Created	☐
YouTube Channel Setup	☐
Filming Equipment	
Video Editing Software	
Video Title	
Video Thumbnail Created	☐
Video Description	
Video Tags	

INSTAGRAM

Once you've mastered Facebook for a while, amp up your reach and engagement with an Instagram account. **Instagram** is a social platform that allows users to post photo and video based content and engage with their followers.

Since Instagram serves the same function as your Facebook **group**, you'll want to refer back to the Facebook group **Posts** lesson to know what type of posts to create.

Also, you can link your Instagram page to your Facebook **Business Manager** and simultaneously manage both of your platform accounts! Refer back to the **Business Manager** section to set one up and then link your Instagram account in your Business Manager settings.

Account Setup

In order to create an Instagram **professional account**, you'll first need a personal account (use your church's name as the 'personal name') by going to **www.instagram.com**

Then, convert the personal account to a professional account by:

- Go to your profile and select the **menu** in the upper right corner
- Select **Settings**

- Select **Account**
- Select **Switch to Professional Account**
- Select **Business**
- You can also link to your Facebook account
- Add **details**
- Click **Done**

Profile photo

Upload a 170 x 170 pixel **profile photo** of your church's logo.

Platform Features

Stories

Just like Facebook stories, Instagram **stories** are temporary (usually 24 hour) photo and video posts designed to share your experiences.

Stories should:

- **Be 1080 x 1920 pixels in size**
- **Show content that will be temporary and will not remain as a post on your page**
  - A time change for tonight's Bible Study
  - Behind-the-scenes of what church staff are like or an event being planned
  - etc.

IGTV

IGTV is Instagram's 'YouTube' experience and can be used to post **1 to 60 minute videos**.

Stories Highlights

Story Highlights are used to archive & categorize old stories for followers to see.

You can create Highlights categories for your general announcements, youth department, behind-the-scenes perspectives, or whatever else you desire to create!

EXERCISE #7

Develop your Instagram strategy.

Account Setup	☐
Profile Photo	☐
Stories Topics	
Stories Image Created	☐
IGTV Topics	
Stories Highlights Categories	

RESOURCES

General

- **Pixel-to-Inch Conversion**
  - *96 Pixels = 1 Inch*
  - Pixel Size ÷ 96 = Inch Size
  - Inch Size x 96 = Pixel Size
- **Google Drive**
  - Allows users to store files on their servers, synchronize files across devices, and share files
- **Google Docs**
  - Brings your documents to life with smart editing and styling tools to help you easily format text and paragraphs
- **Google Sheets**
  - A spreadsheet program created by Google
- **Google Slides**
  - A slideshow presentation program created by Google
- **Google Forms**
  - Create & analyze surveys or registration forms using Google's survey administration app
- **Google Drawings**
  - Create charts, diagrams, logos, and more in Google's free diagramming software

- **Adobe Photoshop**
  - A raster graphics editor for photo editing & compositing, digital painting, animation, and graphic design
- **Adobe Illustrator**
  - Create logos, icons, sketches, typography and other vector art with this vector graphics editor
- **Unsplash**
  - Beautiful, free images and photos that you can download and use for any project
- **Canva**
  - Create perfectly-sized social media graphics, presentations, posters, book covers, calendars, and other visual content
- **Photopea**
  - A free online photo editor similar to Adobe Photoshop that lets you edit photos, apply effects, filters, add text, crop or resize pictures
- **Gravit Designer**
  - A free online vector graphic editor similar to Adobe Illustrator that allows you to create logos, icons, typography, and more like a professional

Style Guide

- **Color Space**
  - Generate nice color palettes, color gradients, & much more
- **Google Fonts**
  - An online library of free licensed fonts

SEO

- **Keywordtool.io**
  - A free online keyword research instrument
- **Moz**
  - SEO software and data to help you increase traffic, rankings, and visibility in search results
- **Backlinko**
  - For next-level SEO training and link building strategies

Websites

- **Wix**
  - Create a stunning website with no coding skills required
- **Typeform**
  - Online form & survey builder
- **Google Pagespeed Insights**
  - Analyzes the content of a web page, then generates suggestions that would make that page faster

- **Google Search Console**
  - Tools and reports help you measure your site's Search traffic and performance, fix issues, and make your site shine in Google Search results
- **Google Analytics**
  - Lets you measure your advertising ROI as well as track your Flash, video, and social networking sites and applications

Facebook & Instagram

- **Profile Photo Template**
  - 170 x 170 pixels
- **Facebook Page Cover Photo Template**
  - 820 x 360 pixels
  - 640 x 312 pixels is safe area
- **Facebook Group Cover Photo Template**
  - 1640 x 856 pixels
  - 1640 x 664 pixels is safe area
- **Post Template**
  - 1080 x 1080 pixels
- **Story Template**
  - 1080 x 1920 pixels
- **Facebook Event Cover Photo Template**
  - 1200 x 628 pixels
- **Facebook Ad Template**
  - 1200 x 628 pixels
- **Facebook Text Overlay Tool**
  - Ensure that the proportion of your ad's text to image ratio isn't too high so your ad can reach its full audience
- **Facebook Business Manager Training**

- **Buffer**
    - Build your audience and grow your brand on social media. Plan and schedule thumb-stopping content that drives meaningful engagement and growth for your accounts

YouTube

- **YouTube Thumbnail Template**
- **YouTube Channel Banner Template**
- **Canon EOS M50 Mirrorless Video Camera**
    - Currently $599 on Amazon
- **BOYA BY-M1000 Condenser Microphone**
    - Currently $125 on Amazon
- **BOYA BY-M1000 3.5mm Electret Condenser Microphone with 1/4" Adapter for Smartphones/iPhone/DSLR/Cameras/PC**
    - Currently $19.88 on Amazon
- **Blender**
    - A free online video editing software available on Windows, Mac, and Linux
- **WeVideo**
    - A collaborative, web-based video editing platform which works in any browser including Google Chrome/Chromebooks
    - Unlimited Plan $15.99/month
- **Adobe Premiere Pro**
    - The industry-leading video editing software for film, TV, and the web
    - $19.99/month with a 7-day free trial

- **Final Cut Pro X**
  - A professional video editing application created by Apple
  - $299.99 total with a 30-day free trial

STAYING UP-TO-DATE

General

- **Pro Church Tools**
  - Explore free tools and resources to help your church continue to reach people beyond your Sunday service
- **Barna Group**
  - A market research firm specializing in studying the religious beliefs and behavior of Americans, and the intersection of faith and culture
- **Nielsen**
  - A global measurement and data analytics company that provides the most complete and trusted view of consumers and markets worldwide

Style Guide

- **Adobe Blog Creative Inspirations & Trends**
  - Annual creative trend forecasts for inspiration

Websites

- **Wix Help Center**

Facebook & Instagram

- **Facebook Help Center**
- **Instagram Help Center**

YouTube

- **YouTube Help Center**
- **YouTube Creator Academy**
  - Education & Courses for YouTube Creators

AUTHOR BIO

Alicia Wyman is a Christian Educator, Deacon, & Digital Designer.

Since 2015, she has been freelancing in the areas of web design, social media marketing, & online advertising as well as consulting for organizations in need of web marketing guidance.

When she's not working, she can be found reading, watching comedies, or spending time with her family.

Alicia lives in Michigan with her husband, Ryan, and their daughter, Blessing.

Made in the USA
Columbia, SC
19 July 2020